THE CHILDREN'S SELF-ESTEEM BOOK

DON'T FEED THE MONSTER ON TUESDAYS!

WRITTEN BY

ADOLPH MOSER
Ed.D.

ILLUSTRATED BY

DAVID MELTON

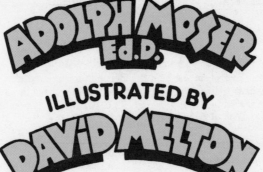

LANDMARK EDITIONS, INC.

P.O. Box 4469   1402 Kansas Avenue   Kansas City, Missouri 64127

Dedicated to
Alex
who has all the signs
of a monster masher.

TEXT: COPYRIGHT © 1991 BY ADOLPH J. MOSER, Ed.D.

ILLUSTRATIONS: COPYRIGHT © 1991 BY DAVID MELTON

International Standard Book Number: 0-933849-38-9 (LIB.BDG.)

Library of Congress Cataloging-in-Publication Data
Moser, Adolph, 1938-
    Don't feed the monster on Tuesdays! : the children's self-esteem book / written by
Adolph J. Moser, illustrated by David Melton.
        p.   cm.
    Summary: Discusses how to develop and maintain healthy self-esteem and a positive
attitude.
ISBN 0-933849-38-9 (lib. bdg.)
    1. Self-respect — Juvenile literature.   [1. Self-respect.]
I. Melton, David, 1934-   ill.   II. Title.
BF697.5.S46M67   1991   158'.1 — dc20   91-12941
                                                               CIP
                                                               AC

Editorial Coordinator: Nancy R. Thatch
Creative Coordinator: David Melton

Printed in the United States of America

Landmark Editions, Inc.
P.O. Box 4469
1402 Kansas Avenue
Kansas City, Missouri 64127
(816) 241-4919

Dear Reader:

I am important to me.

I want to feel good about myself, to like myself, and to enjoy being me.

I need to know that other people like me, and love me, and care about me.

I am pleased when I do things well. I like for people to tell me when I've done something right.

I know some people can do some things better than I can. But most of the time, I try to do my very best. When I make improvements, I am pleased.

I love my wife and my children, and I enjoy being with them.

I care about other people, too, and I try to help them when they are in trouble.

I am not a United States senator, or a superstar, or a major league baseball player. But I am an important person. And I have a strong sense of self-esteem.

You are an important person too. Your self-esteem is important to you. So I wrote this book just for you.

— Your Friend,
Adolph Moser

P.S. Ask your parents to read this book too.

It happens every day.
Some people look
in their mirrors
and scream —

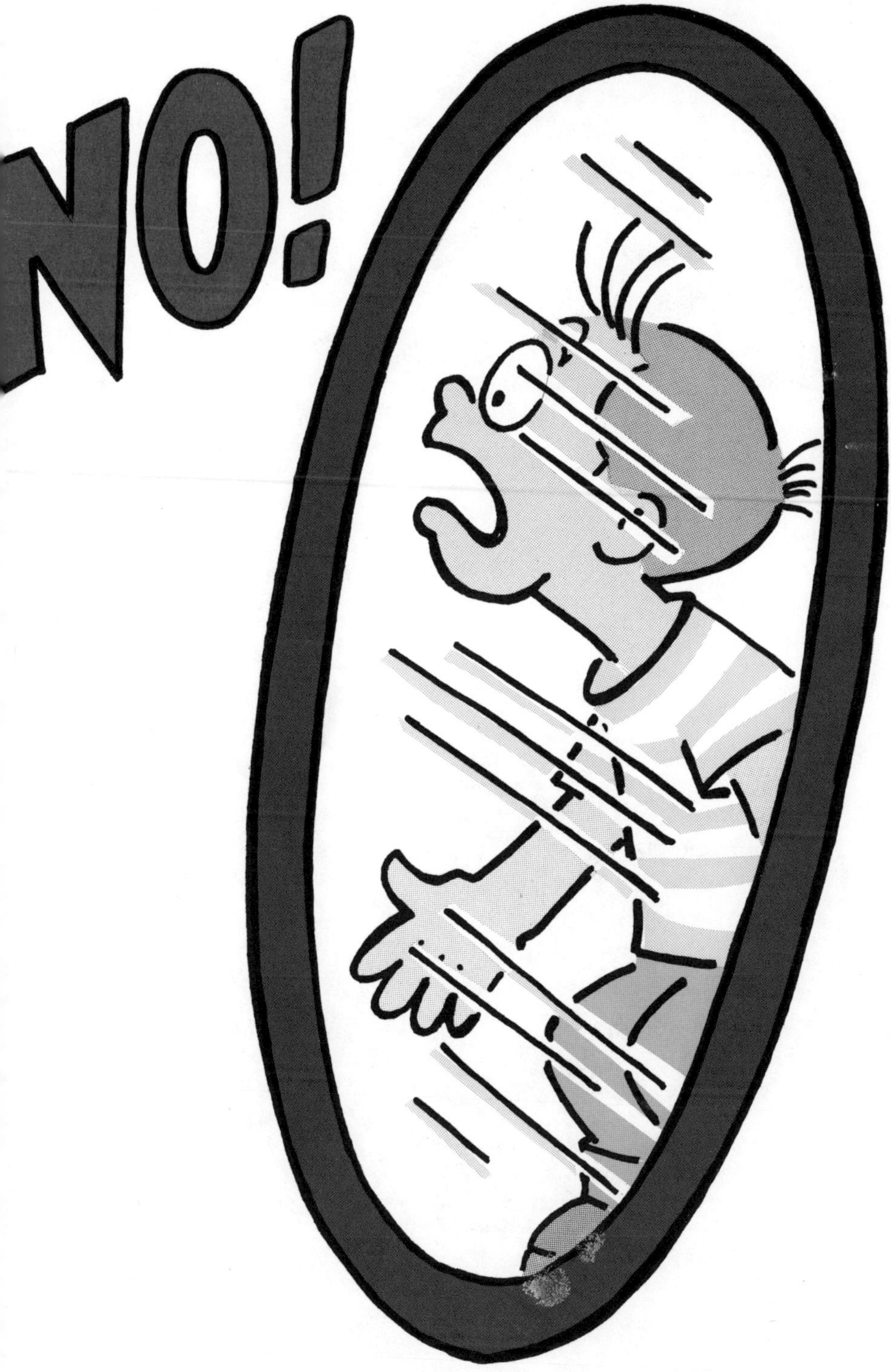
NO!

"My nose is too long!"

"My ears are too big!"

8

"My eyes are too small!"

"My mouth is too wide!"

9

"I am too tall!"

"I am too short!"
10

"I am too fat!"

"I am too skinny!"

"I think I look like a nerd!"

11

Many children,
and adults, too,
are picky, picky, picky
about the way they look.

They don't like other things
about themselves either.

"I don't make high grades in school.
I must be dumb."

"And I'm too shy to talk to people.
I guess I'm stupid."

13

"My classmates don't like me
as much as they do the other kids.
Something must be wrong with me."

"My parents scold me.
So maybe they don't love me."

"Sometimes I spill things.
I'm just too clumsy."

"Sometimes I do things I shouldn't.
Maybe I'm a bad person."

15

If you ever think such things,
you are not alone.

All children,
both boys and girls,
have these thoughts.

And adults,
both men and women,
think them too.

Why do we think such things
about ourselves?

Well—
somewhere inside our brains
there is an area
that makes us think
negative thoughts.

It's as if we have
a little green monster
inside our heads
who is determined to
make us feel bad
about ourselves.

That little monster
is really a sly one.
He begins his attacks
by whispering
awful things to us.

If we LISTEN to
his whispers,
the monster's voice becomes
louder and LOUDER!

If we BELIEVE the things
the monster tells us,
we lose our self-confidence,
and we become very unhappy.

That monster is
HUNGRY! HUNGRY! HUNGRY!
all the time!

He likes nothing better
than to take great big bites
out of your self-esteem.

Your self-esteem
is how you feel
about yourself.

People who feel good about themselves
and like themselves
have a strong sense of self-esteem.

People who feel bad about themselves
and don't like themselves
have a weak sense of self-esteem.

People with strong self-esteems
have more confidence in themselves;
they make better decisions;
and they are happy most of the time.

Our self-esteem is important
in keeping us healthy too.

People who have
weak self-esteems
are frequently on the sick list.

But people who have
strong self-esteems
don't get sick as often.

And when they do,
they usually get well faster.

So where does a person get
a strong sense of self-esteem?

You can't buy it at the supermarket,
and it's not on sale at the shopping mall.

You start getting
some of your self-esteem
when your mom and dad
tell you they love you.

You get
a little more self-esteem
when other people
say they like you.

You also get self-esteem
when you do something well—

such as making
a good grade at school

or winning a race.

When you are
pleased with yourself,
your self-esteem
grows, and grows, and GROWS!

34

And if you want to keep
your self-esteem strong,
be sure you . . .

DON'T FEED THE MONSTER!

That monster grew
ONE DAY AT A TIME,
and within yourself,
you have the power
to make him shrink
ONE DAY AT A TIME.

And here's how you can do just that—

Start by choosing
one day out of the week—
let's say, Tuesday.

Next Tuesday
make a sign that reads—

DON'T FEED
THE
MONSTER
ON
TUESDAYS!

Then . . .
Hang that sign in your room.

On Tuesday
—all day long—
DON'T FEED THE MONSTER!
Don't let him munch
on your self-esteem,
and don't listen
to his whispers.

Instead—

SAY ONLY NICE THINGS to yourself.

When you SAY NICE THINGS to yourself,
you'll start feeling better about yourself.
UP goes your self-esteem!
And DOWN goes the monster!

If you want your parents
to say they love you more often,
then tell them you
love them more often.

When they say
they love you, too,
UP goes your self-esteem!
And DOWN goes the monster!

40

And if you want more people
to like you,
you can make that happen too.

All you have to do
is BE FRIENDLY
and SAY NICE THINGS
to more people.

When you say nice things
to more people,
then more people will like you.

As more people like you,
you will find that
you like yourself even better.

UP goes your self-esteem!
And DOWN goes the monster!

43

If you have an accident,
and the monster says,
"SHAME! SHAME! SHAME!"

don't come unglued!
It was only an accident,
and everyone has accidents,
even parents, and teachers too.

44

If you make a mess of things,
that doesn't mean you're a bad person.
The truth is, you're a good person
who happened to make a mistake.

Just say, "I'm sorry,"
then clean up the mess,
and try not to make
the same mistake again.

45

If you have trouble understanding
some of your school lessons,
you may need extra help.
There's nothing wrong with that.
Everyone needs help sometime.

Smart people ask for help
when they need it.
SO DO THE SMART THING!
Tell your teachers and parents
that you need their help.

When you ask for help,
your teachers and parents
will know you want to learn more,
and they will help you.

As you learn more,
you'll feel proud of yourself.
UP goes your self-esteem!
And DOWN goes the monster!

You may want
to be the best
at anything you try.
But you must realize that
some people can do some things
better than you can.

It's not important that
you win every race.

What is important
is that you always try
to do your very best.

When you know you've done
your very best,
UP goes your self-esteem!
And DOWN goes the monster!

If you want to build
a stronger self-esteem,
you must become
a friend to yourself.

If you try,
you can become
your own best friend.

Best friends like each other.

SO LIKE YOURSELF!

Best friends forgive each other's mistakes.

SO FORGIVE YOURSELF!

Best friends are kind to each other.

SO BE KIND TO YOURSELF!

I AM A NICE KID, A GOOD THINKER, AND REALLY FRIENDLY!

If you can go the whole day
on Tuesday
without feeding the monster,
your self-esteem
will be **ONE DAY STRONGER**,
and the monster
will be one day weaker.

If you can think only
good thoughts about yourself
all day Tuesday,
it will be easier
for you to think
nice things about yourself
on Wednesday.

Do the same thing on Thursday,
and Friday will be even easier.
And before you know it,
your self-esteem will be so strong
and the monster will be so weak
that you will no longer
hear his tiny voice.
Then you will be able to enjoy
a new and much happier you.